BIG thoughts for Little minds

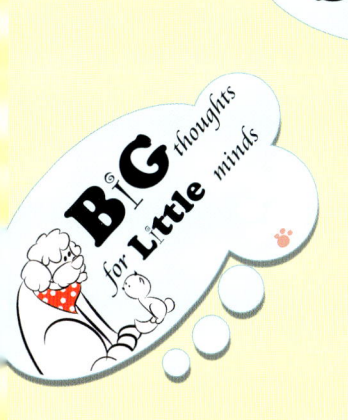

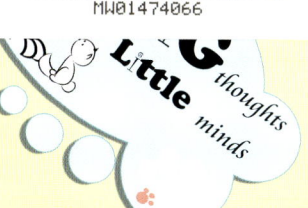

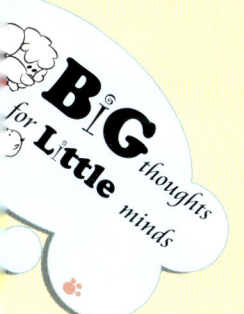

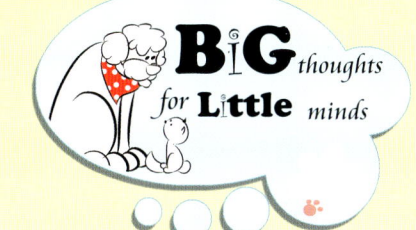

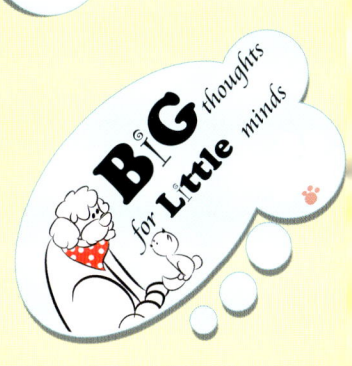

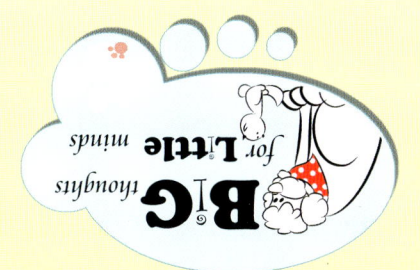

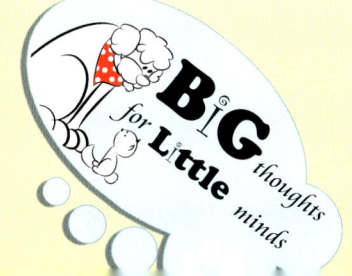

A **BiG** thoughts for **Little** minds Production

ACKNOWLEDGMENTS:

TEXT: Ivan Gouveia, based on Matthew 6, verses 9-13, the Bible.
ILLUSTRATIONS: Leilen Basan
DESIGN: Leilen Basan, M-A Mignot

ISBN: 978-1-63264-053-6

© 2015 Ivan Gouveia and Leilen Basan.

All Rights Reserved.

Published by Book Barn Publishing.

Printed in China.

HOW DO I Pray?

BASED ON MATTHEW 6, VERSES 9–13

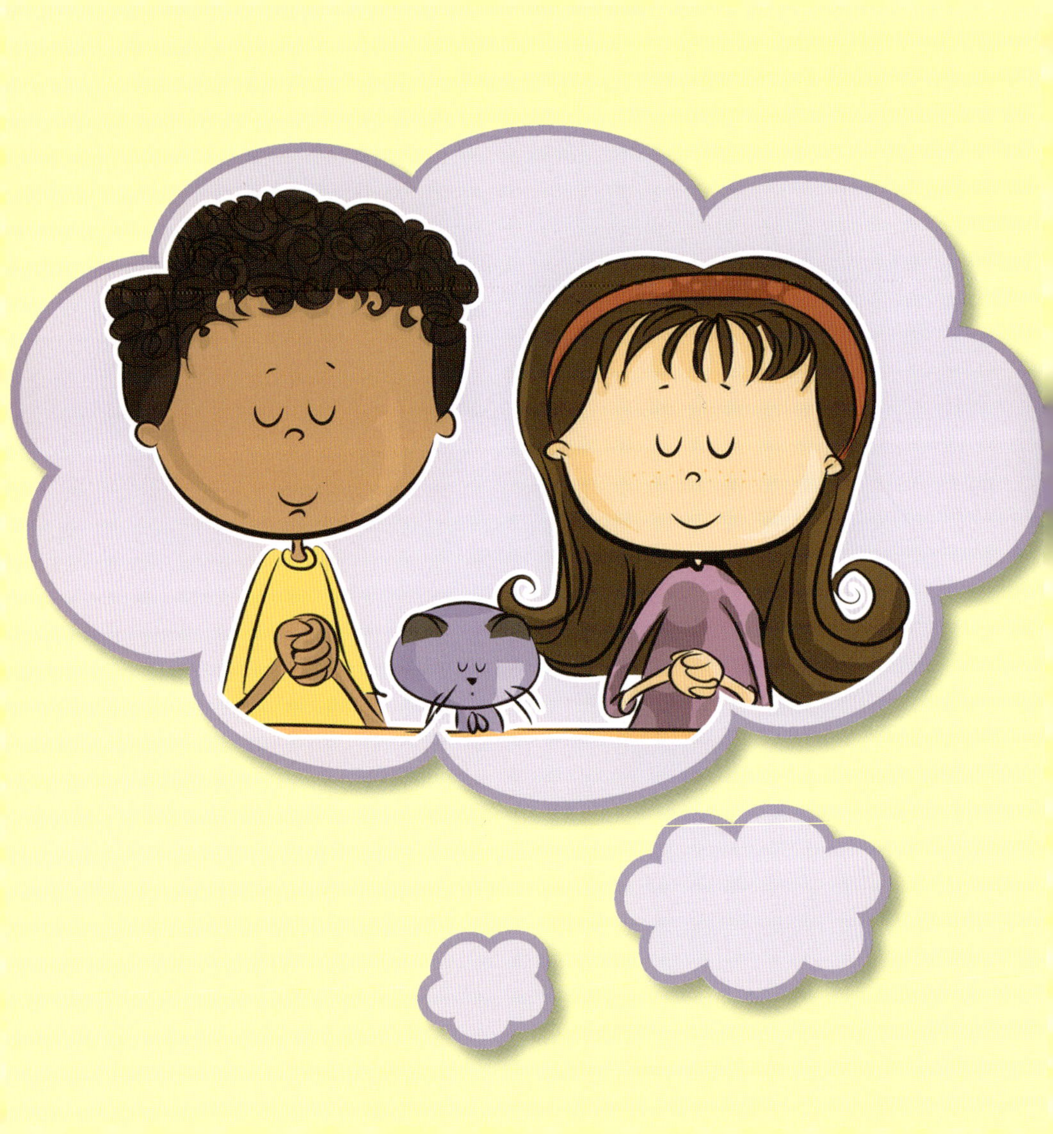

Dedicated to:

"Baby Campbell"

2023

From:

Grandma's friend Janice

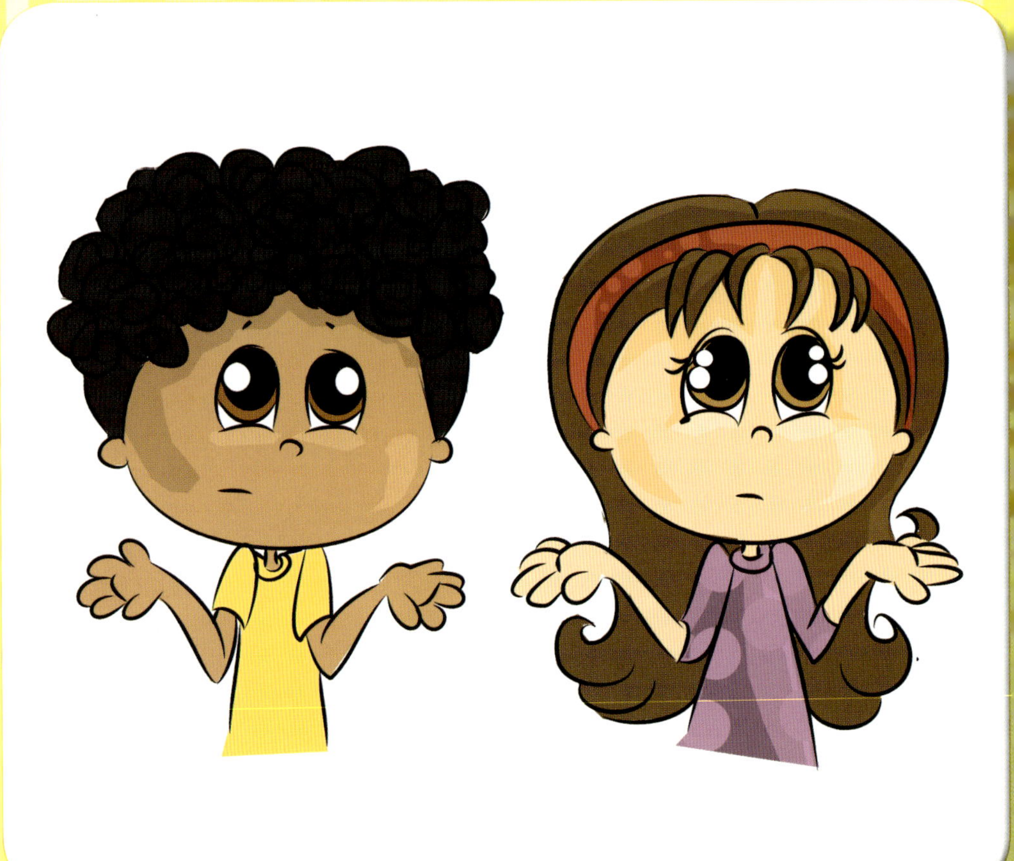

Have you ever wanted to pray to God, but you weren't sure what were the right words to say?

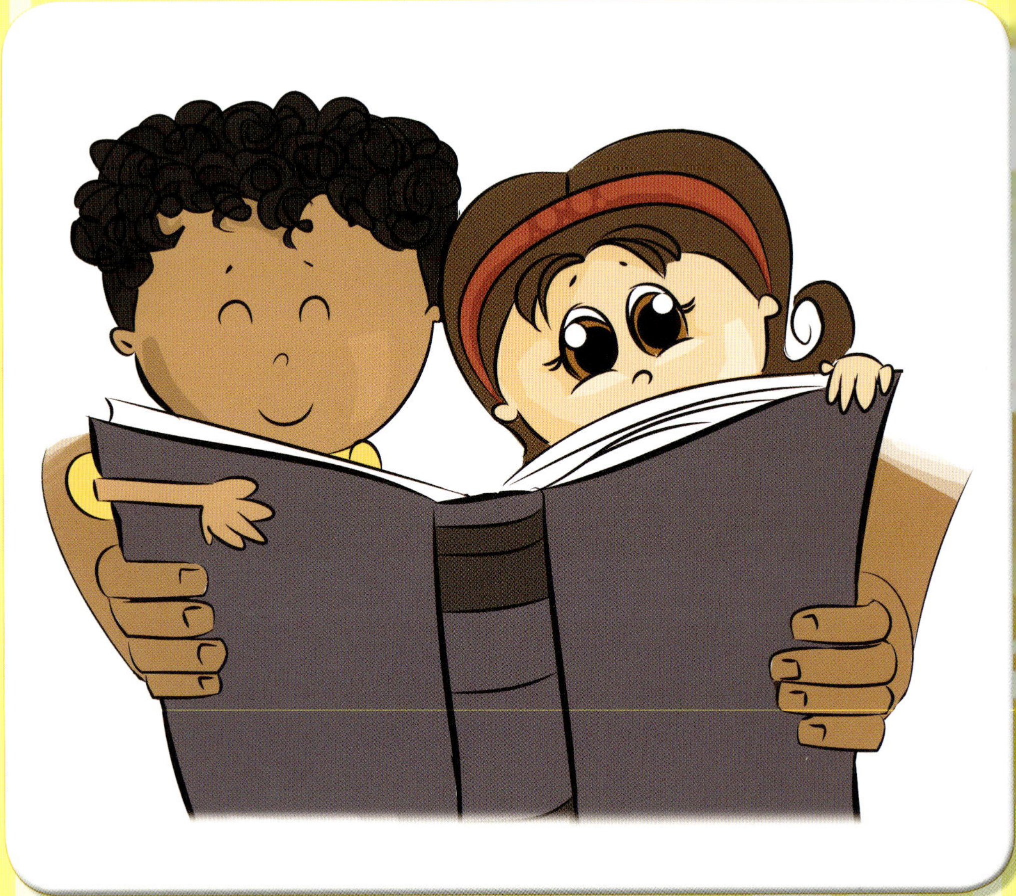

Here is a prayer that my daddy prayed with me. It comes from the Bible. It is the prayer that Jesus, God's Son, taught His friends to pray when they weren't sure how to pray either.

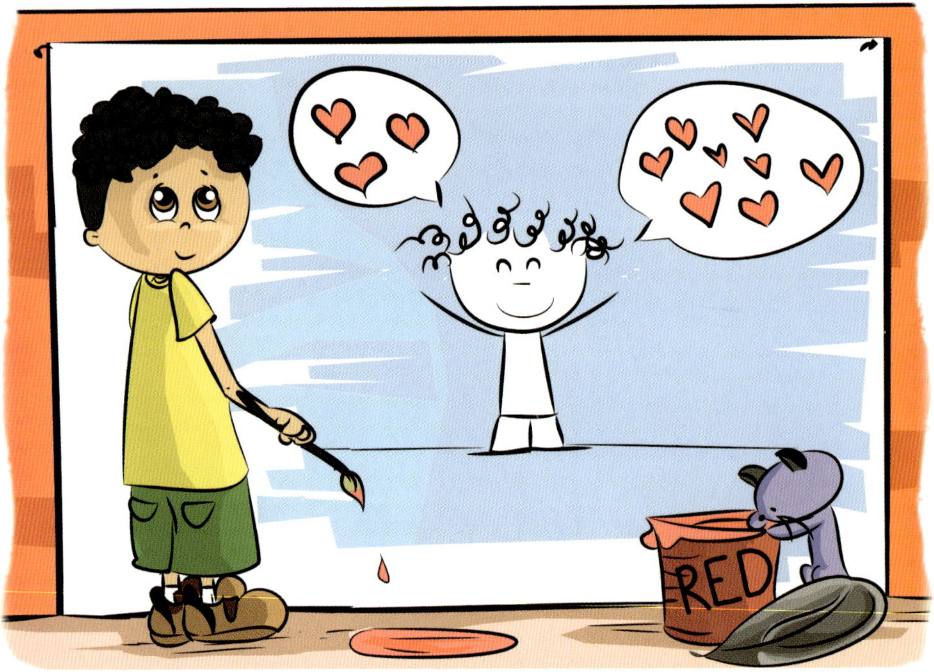
RED

I am not sure if I remember it all, but it goes something like this:

Dear Father, who lives in heaven above, this is _____, Your child. You are everything that is perfect and true. Help me remember to praise You.

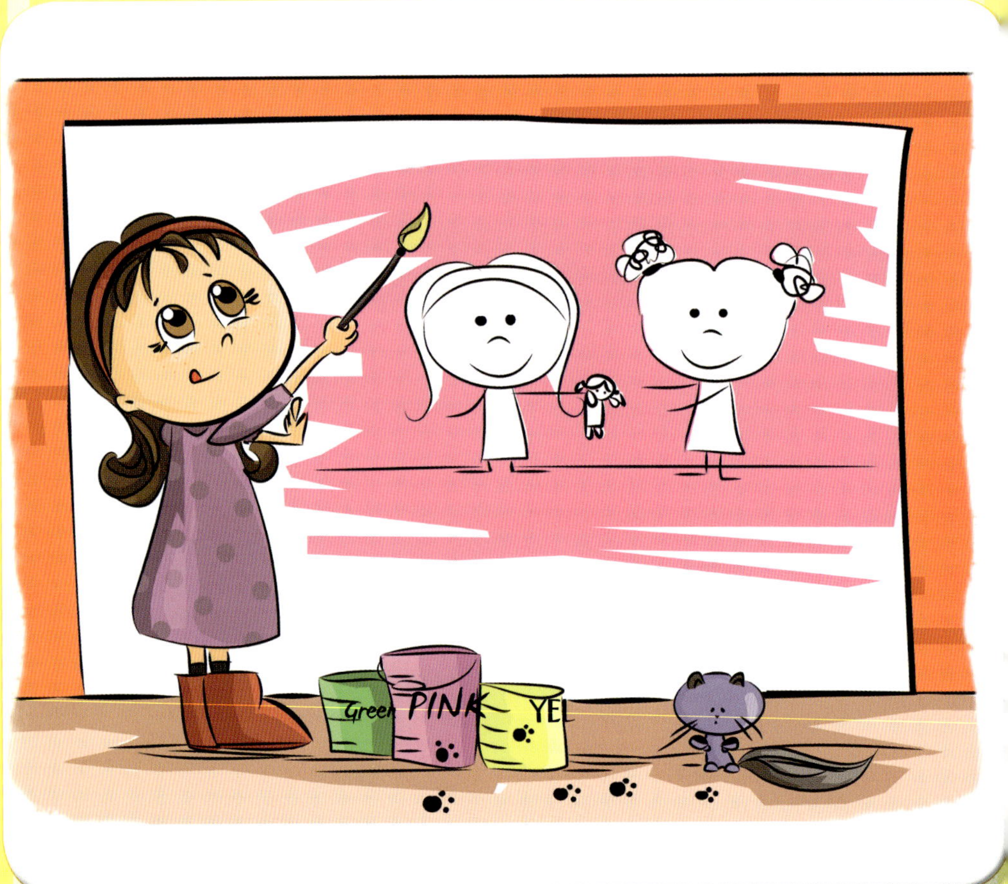
Green
PINK
YEL

I want to live with You in heaven some day, where everything is bright and beautiful. But until I get there, I want Your heavenly spirit to live in me, so that I can be an example of Your love now, and for all eternity.

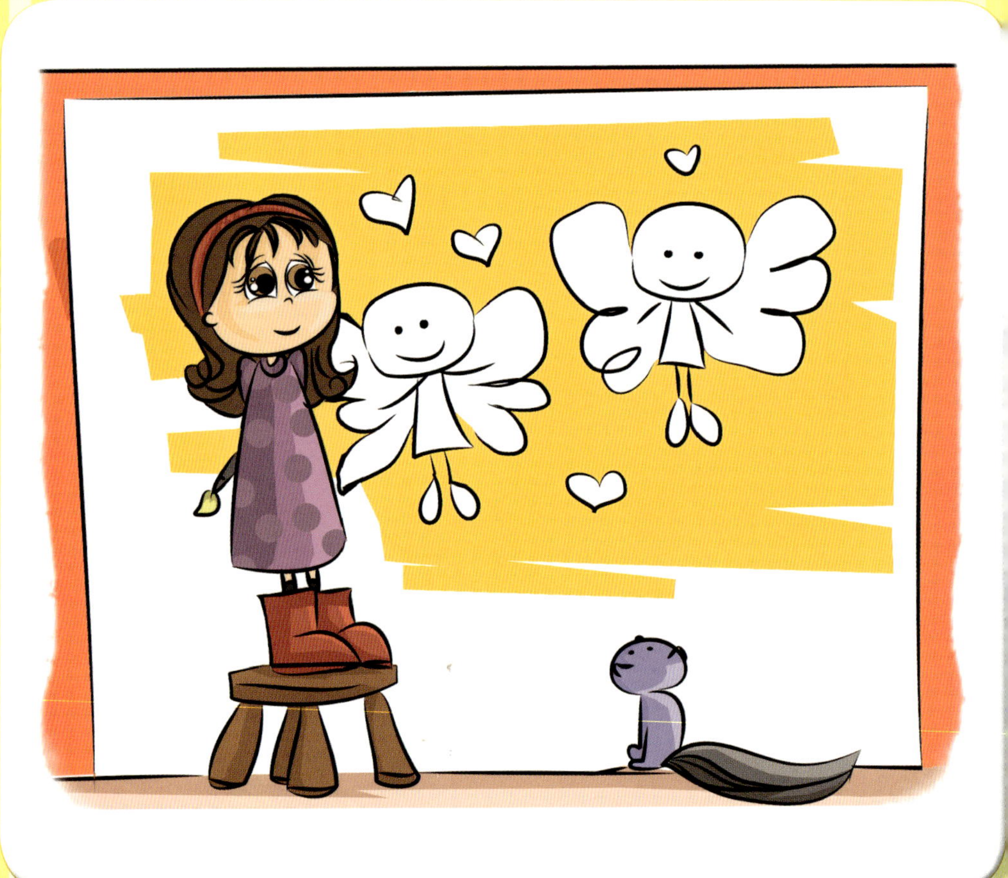

Even though I am still here on Planet Earth, I want to follow Your voice and do what You ask me to do. Help me not to be selfish and mean to others. Rather, help me to be more like the angels in heaven, who reflect Your love and light.

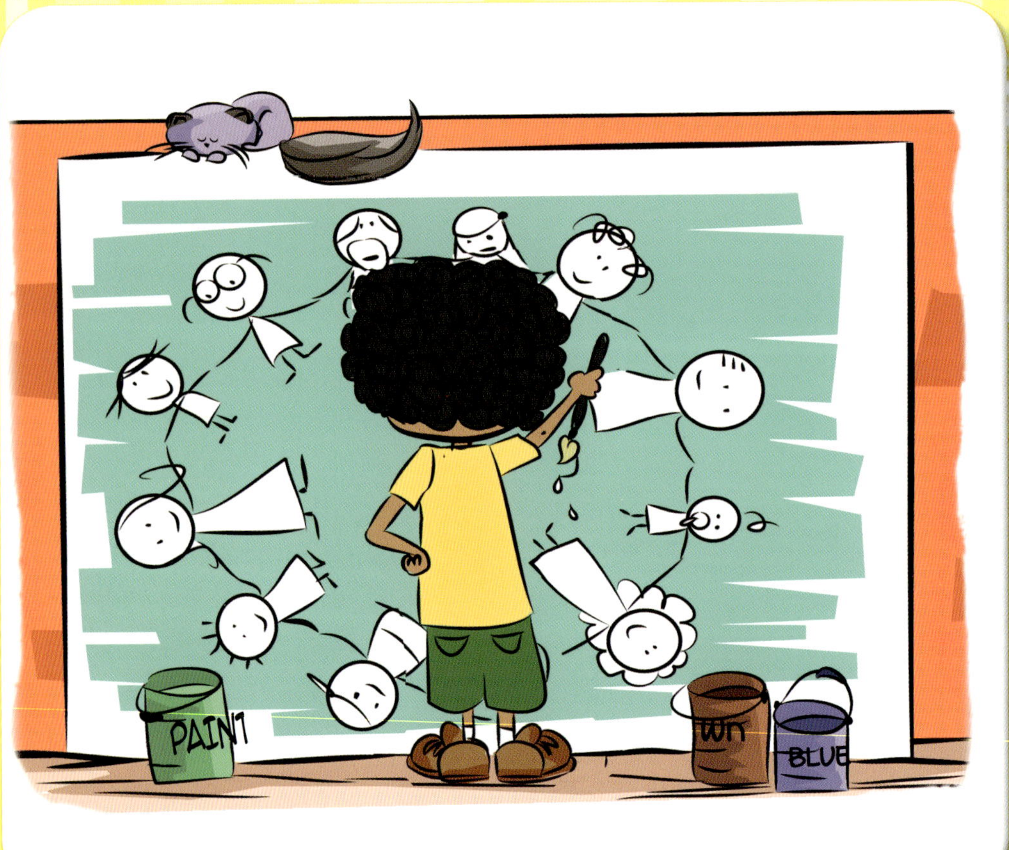
PAINT
BLUE

Please supply all of our needs, not only for me and my family, but for every daddy, mommy, brother, sister, son, and daughter in the world.

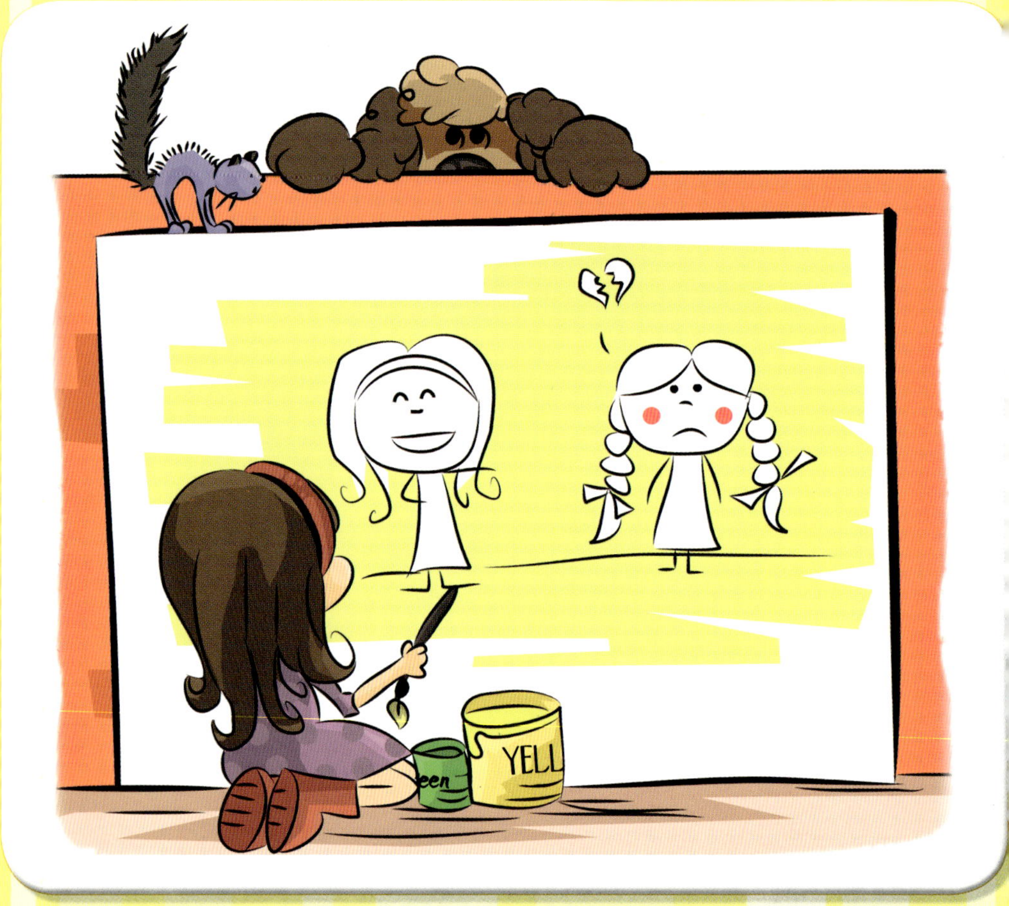
een
YELL

Please forgive me for the wrong things that I have done. I don't want to hurt You or others, but I know that sometimes I do. Please help me to make things better by asking others for forgiveness, and trying hard not to make the same mistakes again.

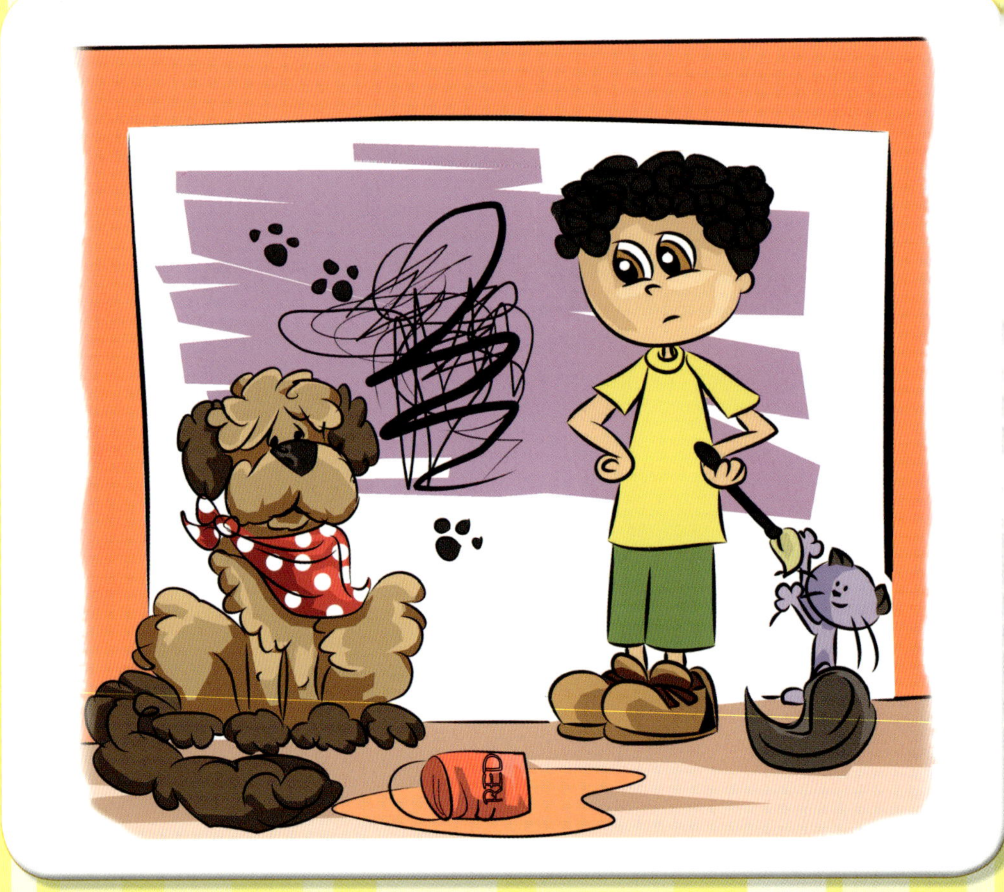
RED

Please help me not to hold a grudge against anyone who has hurt me. Help me to forgive others as You always forgive me.

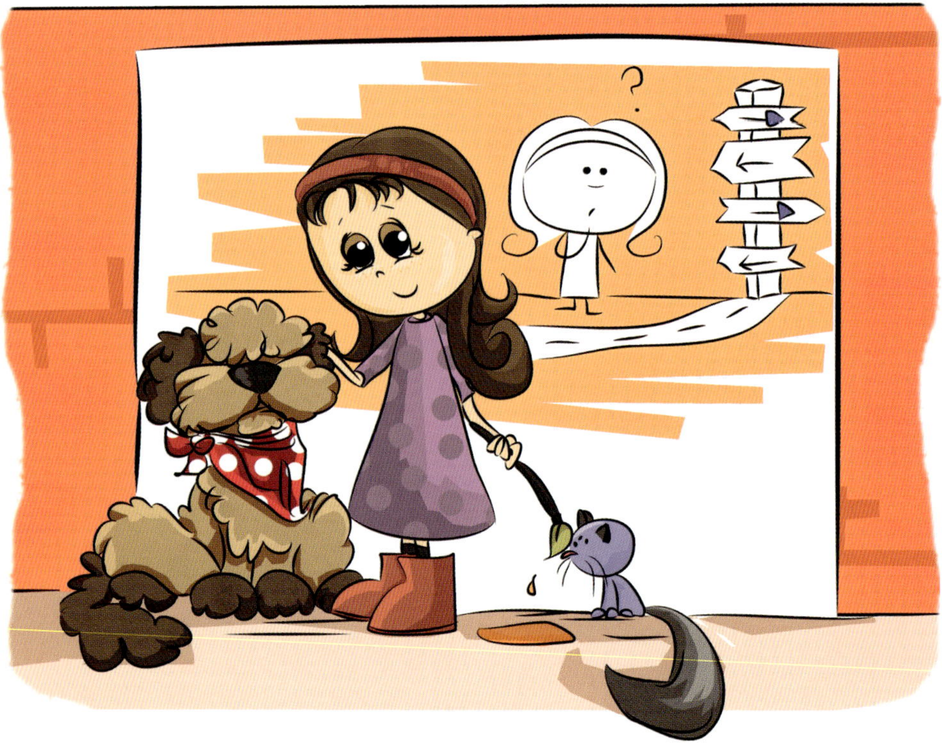

There are many choices I have to make in my life every day. What choice should I make? Sometimes I am quite confused. Help me to resist the wrong choices, and to choose to do what is right, so that I can draw closer to You.

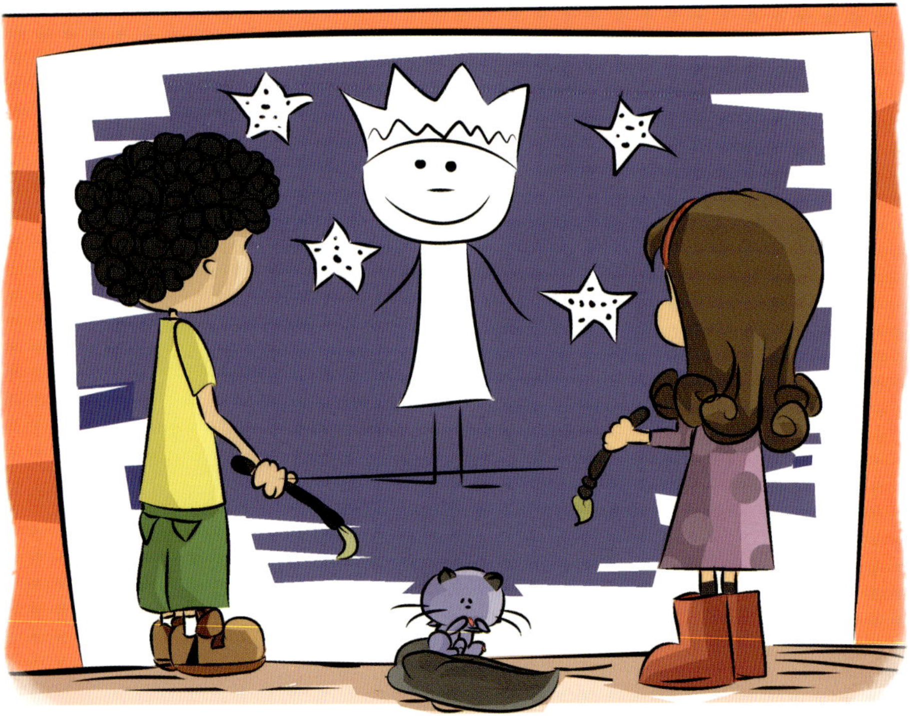

I love You! I acknowledge that You are the king of all things. You are the most powerful being in the whole universe, and from You all good things come.

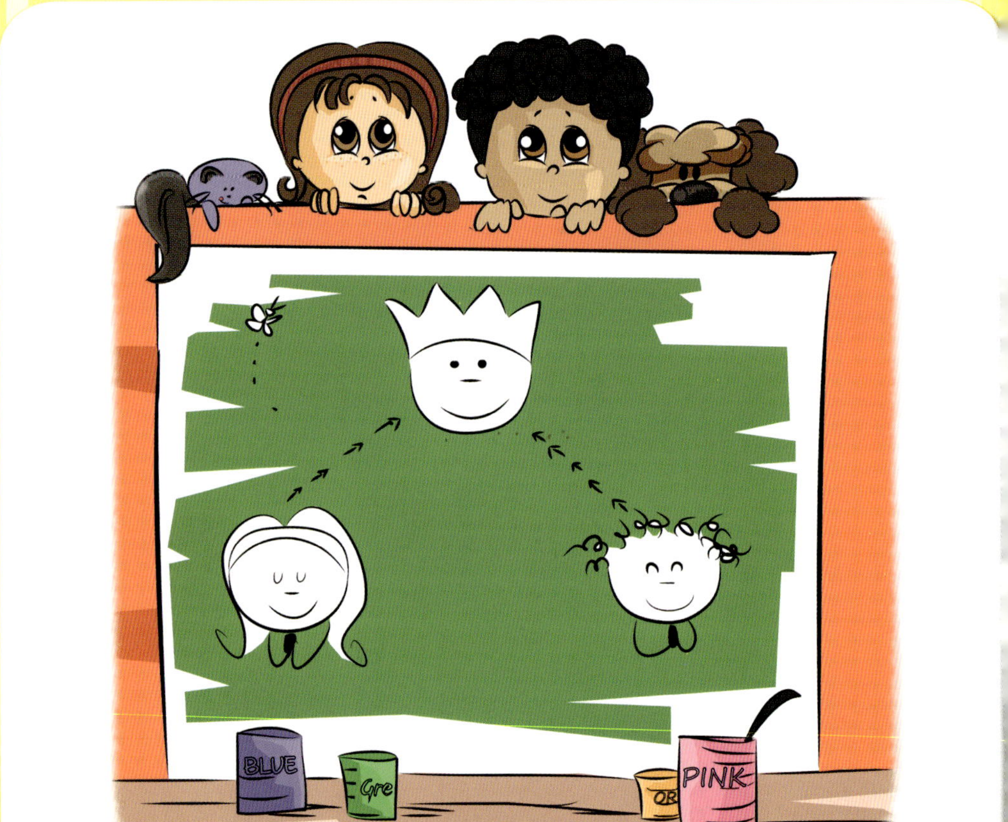
BLUE
Gre
OR
PINK

I know You will hear this prayer and answer it. For this I am forever grateful.
Amen.

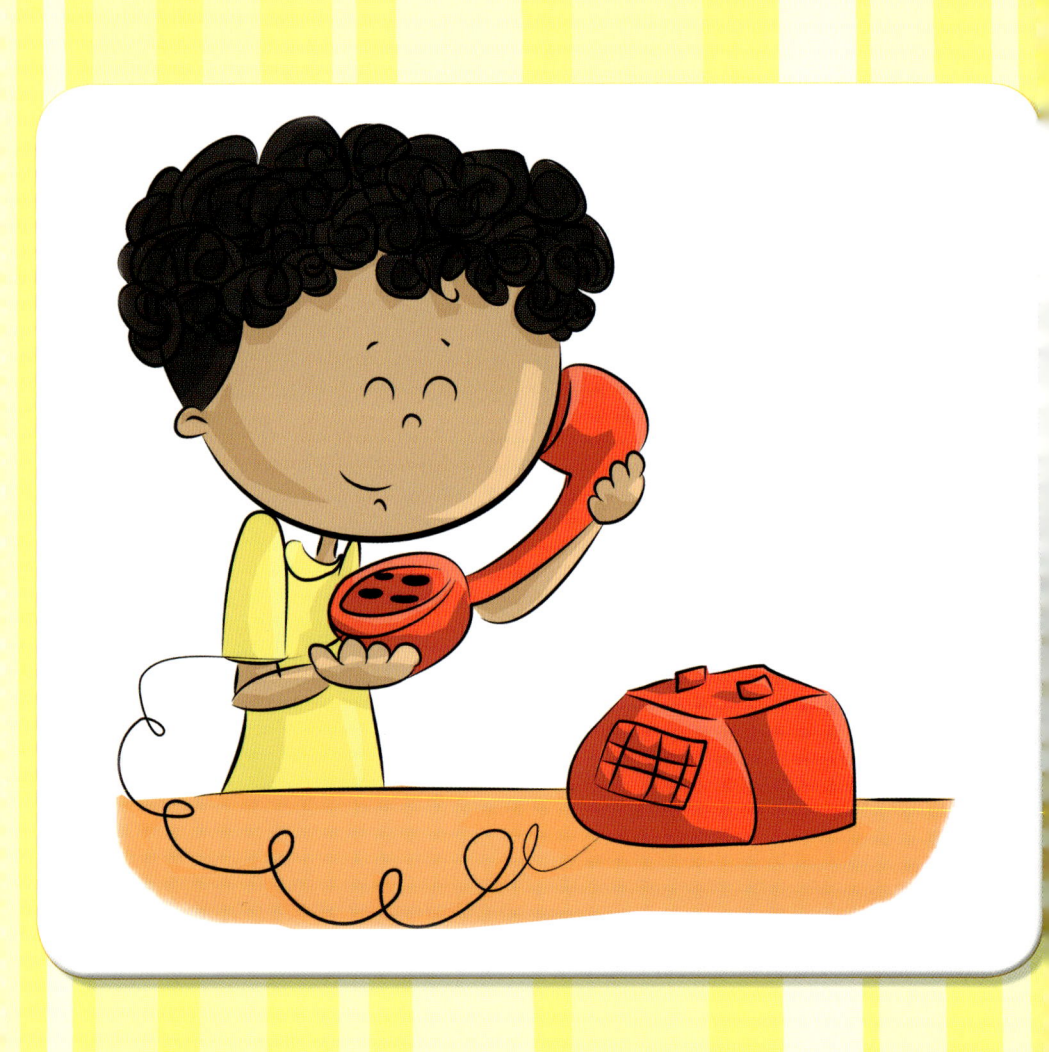

Prayer is like talking to your dad when you want to ask him for something. What's more special, though, is that when we talk to God, we are talking to the God of the whole universe, who is all-powerful and takes care of everyone. He can do anything for us!

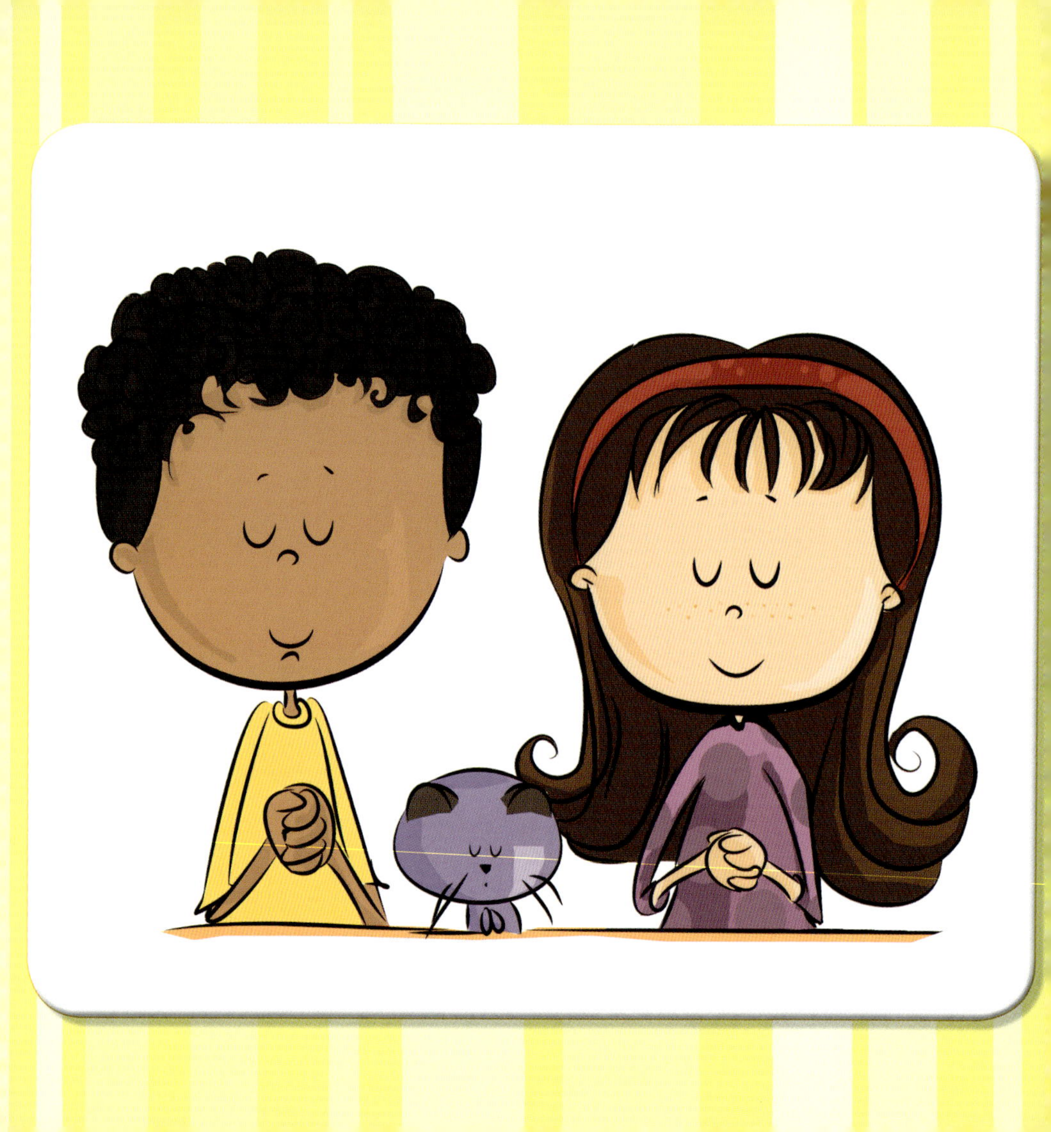

Nothing is impossible for God! You can pray to Him too. And if you don't remember these words, just say what comes from your heart. Have fun praying! It never fails.

My big thoughts!

1 Do you remember the first time you ever prayed to God?

2 Do you know any prayers by heart? If you don't, ask your mommy or daddy to teach you some.

3 Can you think of some of the awesome things God does for you that you can thank Him for?

4 Have you ever imagined what it will be like in heaven? What would you wish to have or do in heaven?

5 Did you know that when we get to heaven we will be like the angels? Try being angelic today.

Think Think Think

6 Do you remember a time when you prayed for something and God answered your prayer?

7 Do you know why it is important to say you are sorry when you make a mistake?

8 When someone makes a mistake that hurts you, do you try to forgive him or her quickly?

9 Do you remember the last time you had to choose between two or more things? Was it easy or difficult to choose?

10 Think about what it would be like to live with God—the king of the whole universe—forever.

11 Did you ever think that prayer could be so fun and simple?

12 Do you feel safe knowing that God is always watching over you and protecting you?

13 Stop now and say a prayer in your own words—whatever comes from your heart.

Think
Think
Think

BIG thoughts for Little minds

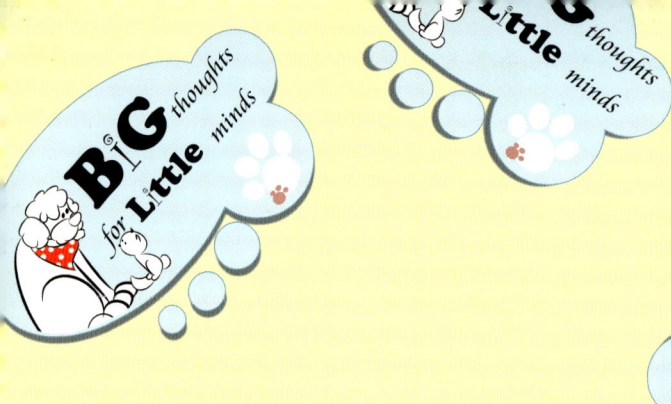

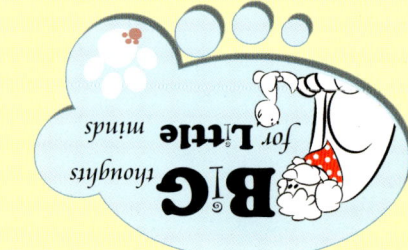

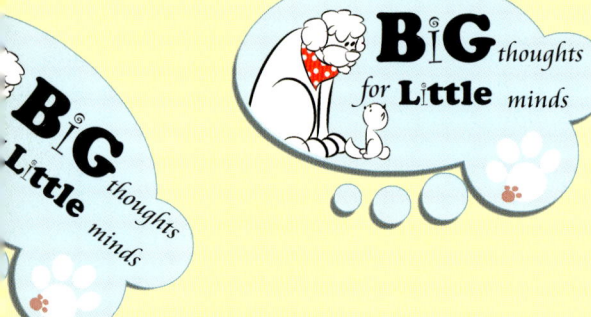

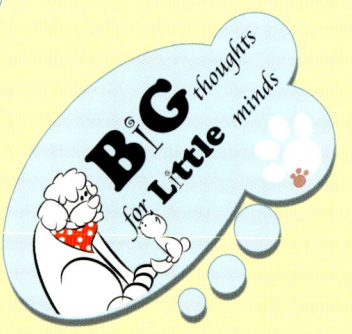

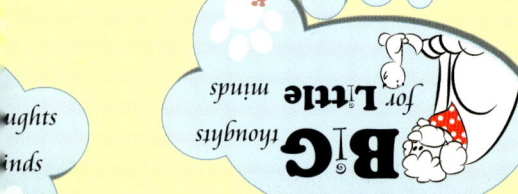